SEATTLE
SOUNDERS FC
SEASON ONE

SEASON ONE

SEATTLE SOUNDERS FC

THE BIRTH OF A
NEW TRADITION

RICHARD MORRISON

CHAD MACK

SASQUATCH BOOKS
SEATTLE

For my wife, Marti, and my children, Yael and Arielle, for their patience, love, and support of my passion. To my special friend Gary Whitted for constant encouragement, and to all my neurosurgical colleagues for reminding me that photography was a healthy pursuit. —Rick Morrison

With love to Dana and Olivia, who inspire me. With respect to coach Tim Moore, who taught me how to play the game with heart. With gratitude to Diane, who encouraged me to pursue my passions. —Chad Mack

Logo, font style, and team uniform for Seattle Sounders FC are registered trademarks and
appear with permission from Seattle Sounders FC.

Printed in Canada
Published by Sasquatch Books
Distributed by PGW/Perseus
15 14 13 12 11 10   9 8 7 6 5 4 3 2 1

Cover photograph: Richard Morrison
Cover design: Rosebud Eustace
Interior photographs: Richard Morrison
Interior design and composition: Rosebud Eustace

Library of Congress Cataloging-in-Publication Data is available.

ISBN-13: 978-1-57061-678-5

Sasquatch Books
119 South Main Street, Suite 400
Seattle, WA 98104
(206) 467-4300
www.sasquatchbooks.com
custserv@sasquatchbooks.com

CONTENTS

ABOUT THE AUTHORS

Richard Morrison—photographer

Dr. Rick Morrison holds the Staatz-endowed Professorship in Neurological Surgery at the University of Washington School of Medicine, and is also an accomplished sports photographer. Through his camera lens, he brings the science of the sport to life with technical clarity. *www.morrisonphotos.com*

Chad Mack—writer

Chad Mack works by day as a communications manager for Microsoft and by night runs a small public relations agency. A soccer enthusiast, Chad coaches youth soccer, captains his over-30 men's team, and sits on the Greater Seattle Soccer League Board. *www.mackmarketing.com*

ACKNOWLEDGMENTS

We thank David Falk, Elizabeth Wales, Greg Roth, Heidi Hutchinson, and Jose Romero for their invaluable partnerships. Special thanks go to Drew Carey, Frank MacDonald, Gary Wright, and Suzanne Lavender, without whom this book would not have been possible.

FOREWORD

Being part of the Sounders FC ownership group has been a dream come true. From the beginning, my commitment has always been to the fans and to giving them a voice, because when it comes right down to it . . . I am a fan. We all are.

Sounders FC fans are something really special. This city has embraced our club. I'll never forget our home opener—from the number of fans gathering together for the March to the Match, to the signs and flags in the stands, to the wall of scarves, to the win. It was a magical night. And it seemed like every match day was a magical one.

Our crowds were big, but just as important, they were involved in the game. With each game, more and more people learned the songs and chants, and the banners seemed to get bigger and bigger.

Throughout the season, we had our share of questionable calls and late-game heroics, but one thing that stayed true was the passion and noise generated every time we took the field.

The players, the coaches, and all members of the organization were happy to share the victories and triumphs with our people, the fans. This was a bit of a storybook season, what with the Sounders winning the U.S. Open Cup, making the playoffs, and setting all kinds of cool records.

We all believed that when you get this many people together who love the game, this kind of success was possible. But you know what? The best is yet to come.

Drew Carey

—Drew Carey,
Seattle Sounders FC Owner & Sounders FC Alliance Chairman

INTRODUCTION

Seattle Sounders FC *season one* marked the birth of a new soccer tradition in Seattle and, to a greater extent, in Major League Soccer (MLS). Seattleites supported their beloved professional soccer teams through two previous iterations, both also called the Sounders, and excitement for the third version had been building since the November 2007 announcement that the new team would join MLS. After conducting a fan vote that preserved the team's historic name, the club set about building an organization it hoped would establish the city as the new home of American soccer.

When inaugural match day finally arrived, a mass of season ticket holders assembled in Seattle's Occidental Park adorned with scarves, outfitted in rave green, and eager to march to the match and sing the songs that soon distinguished them as the preeminent supporters in the league. As the season unfolded, these fans were treated to world-class exhibitions with Chelsea FC and FC Barcelona, presented a U.S. Open Cup Championship trophy, and invited to an MLS Cup. How could *season two* possibly top that? Sounders FC supporters can't wait to find out.

On January 21, 2009, two months before the team's MLS debut, the Seattle Sounders FC entered training camp at the Virginia Mason Athletic Center, home of the Seattle Seahawks, in Renton, Washington. The historic day marked the genesis of the team that would go on to win the 2009 U.S. Open Cup Championship and become the first expansion team since 1998 to compile a winning regular-season record and qualify for the MLS Cup playoffs. But before reaching these milestones, the 36 players in attendance were scrutinized by head coach Sigi Schmid, who was tasked with setting the 24-man inaugural season squad. There were familiar faces among the aspiring group of Sounders—most notably goalkeeper Kasey Keller, who had returned to his home state from a storied career abroad, and former Arsenal star Freddie Ljungberg. Others were unknown, some had not yet arrived in camp, and many were Sounders United Soccer League First Division (USL-1) hopefuls vying for coveted roster spots. Just nine days later, five players had fallen, and the refined team set off for further training in Buenos Aires by way of Southern California.

GENESIS

The first Sounders FC training session
begins with calisthenics.

Patrick Ianni (front), a member of the 2008 U.S. Olympic Team, was acquired from the Houston Dynamo on January 26, 2009. He joined camp and is shown here being defended by former Sounders USL-1 player Roger Levesque.

Former Sounder and 2007 USL-1 MVP Sebastien Le Toux entered training camp knowing his fate. Sounders FC signed Le Toux as its first player on May 7, 2008. Here, Le Toux is tackled by another former USL-1 Sounder, Zach Scott.

Hoping to join the inaugural Sounders FC team, these players jog during warm-ups.

Sounders FC technical director Chris Henderson assists the general manager, Adrian Hanauer, in all areas of soccer operations, including scouting.

Former USL-1 Sounders head coach Brian Schmetzer joined Sounders FC following seven seasons and two USL-1 championships, in 2005 and 2007. Here, he leans in to share insight with new Sounders FC head coach, Sigi Schmid.

Sounders FC selected Wake Forest graduate Evan Brown with its 16th overall pick in the 2009 MLS SuperDraft.

LEFT: Fredy Montero jumps to block a pass during training. Sounders FC signed Montero on loan from his native Colombian team, Atlético Huila.

Goalkeeper Kasey Keller goes airborne during a training session. Keller, a four-time World Cup participant with the United States Men's National Soccer Team and one of the first American goalkeepers to start in the English Premier League and German Bundesliga, signed with Sounders FC on August 14, 2008.

LEFT: Keller is a local boy who made good, growing up in Olympia, Washington, and playing collegiate soccer at the University of Portland.

When I started my career in Europe, I always said that I wanted to finish playing back at home in the U.S. I wasn't sure that dream was ever going to come true. I still can't believe it's a reality.

—*Kasey Keller*

Rookie Steve Zakuani runs a speed test during training. Zakuani led the NCAA Division I in scoring with 20 goals in 2008.

Former San Jose Earthquake James Riley closely defends Steve Zakuani during scrimmage.

Former USL-1 Sounders player Taylor Graham faces off against former Houston Dynamo Nate Jaqua.

Brad Evans passes to a teammate during scrimmage. Evans began his MLS career in 2007 with the Columbus Crew under Sigi Schmid, current Sounders FC coach. Together they won the 2008 MLS Championship. Sounders FC selected Evans in the 2008 MLS Expansion Draft and were pleased to have him in training camp.

He's an exciting central player. I think he was a very big part of Columbus's championship run. He can score. He's a competitor. He has a great desire to improve as a player.

—*Chris Henderson, Sounders FC technical director*

The orange scrimmage team returns a goal following a small-sided scrimmage match.

OPPOSITE: Cuban midfielder Osvaldo Alonso reflects on the day of training.

It's great to get a player like Alonso. As a technical central midfielder, he's very good with the ball, a clever passer, and he's coming off a very successful USL season.

—*Head coach Sigi Schmid*

At the end of the first Sounders FC practice, players gather around to hear head coach Schmid's impressions on the day and, in some cases, to learn their fate.

A city steeped in soccer tradition, Seattle eagerly awaited the March 19, 2009, debut of its new MLS franchise. Sounders FC represented the third incarnation of the fans' beloved Sounders, born first in 1974 to the North American Soccer League (NASL) and then reborn 20 years later in 1994 to the United Soccer League (USL) First Division. By gobbling up 22,000 inaugural season ticket packages before the opening kickoff and casting 15,000 votes in the club's "name the team" promotion to preserve the Sounders name, the fans became the story on that debut night. Outfitted with their inaugural season scarves, the enthusiastic supporters flooded into Qwest Field and were rewarded with a compelling 3-0 win over the New York Red Bulls before a sellout crowd of 32,523. At the end of the evening, it was clear that the tradition had been born yet again, and the third time would be the charm.

SOUNDERS FC DEBUT

When one door closes, many will open. It's hard to see the Sonics moving on as they have, but this is something new on the horizon that many people can rally around, and I'm enthused to be a part of [it].

—*Kevin Calabro*

In July 2008 Seattle's NBA team, the SuperSonics, finalized a move to Oklahoma City for its 2008–09 season, and the Sounders FC stepped in to fill the void. The connection was made even more clear when the Seattle Sonics "voice," Kevin Calabro, was named as the Sounders FC play-by-play announcer.

Sounders FC majority owner Joe Roth (left) shares a moment with owner Drew Carey before the debut match.

The Seattle Sounders FC marching band, Sound Wave, leads fans to Qwest Field in the "March to the Match" from nearby Occidental Park before settling into the stands.

An inaugural match wouldn't be quite the
same without cheerleaders—at least in
America.

Washington Governor Christine Gregoire
bestows the first ceremonial Golden
Scarf to MLS Commissioner Dan Garber,
establishing a unique Sounders FC
tradition.

Drew Carey fires up the crowd on opening
night while (left to right) Adrian Hanauer,
Governor Gregoire, Commissioner Garber,
and Joe Roth look on.

Sounders FC supporters display the green scarves that came with their season ticket packages. This dramatic visual display of support was an integral part of every home match.

Referee: Jair Marrufo
Assistants: Corey Rockwell, Fabio Tovar
Fourth: Terry Vaughn

The teams are led out onto the pitch by
the referee crew in charge of the 2009
inaugural season opener.

Dr. Stephen Michael Newby leads the singing of the national anthem before each home match. Newby is director of the Center for Worship and University Ministries at Seattle Pacific University.

New York Red Bulls and Seattle Sounders
FC players pose for a photo before kickoff.

It's noisier here because we have more fans. Comparing both atmospheres, I'd have to go with Seattle, definitely. Thirty-some-thousand fans screaming definitely trumps twenty thousand fans screaming.

—*Tyrone Marshall*

Tyrone Marshall, Sounders FC defender #14, gazes up into the south end of the Qwest Field stands. The Emerald City Supporters Group (ECS) populates the south (or Brougham End) of the stadium. The group's colorful flags, banners, and songs rally support for their team.

Before being traded to Seattle, Marshall spent the past two seasons playing for Toronto FC, whom Sounders FC surpassed for season ticket–sales supremacy upon its debut into the league.

Sounders FC forward Nate Jaqua leaps over Red Bulls goalkeeper Danny Cepero.

Sounders FC head coach Sigi Schmid keeps a watchful eye during the team's debut match.

Sounders FC goalkeeper Kasey Keller springs to cover the crossbar as a shot sails over.

First, [I] thank God for the opportunity, but also [I] thank the entire team and the coaches and the fans for their support. Obviously, this is the start of big things. Now, be prepared for even more.

—*Fredy Montero*

Sounders FC forward Fredy Montero pumps his fist to celebrate his first MLS goal. After the match, Montero commented on the experience and accurately foretold the future. Montero went on to lead the team with 12 goals scored in the 2009 regular season.

Sounders FC forward Roger Levesque entered the match replacing Fredy Montero in the 89th minute.

I took Fredy out at end of game for two reasons: I wanted [Roger], who has been with the Sounders a long time, to be able to say he got in the first game, and also, as I told Fredy, wanted him to hear the crowd . . . and hear the fans and [their] appreciation.

—*Head coach Sigi Schmid*

Sounders FC midfielder Sebastien Le Toux assisted Fredy Montero's first MLS goal in the 12th minute of the match.

Sounders FC midfielder Sanna Nyassi made his MLS debut by starting the match, then gave way for Steve Zakuani, who made his MLS debut in the 68th minute.

Sounders FC midfielder Freddie Ljungberg watches quietly from the sidelines. The Sounders FC designated player and Swedish international star would return from a hip injury and offseason surgery to make his debut the following week versus Real Salt Lake.

Obviously everybody, from the players and the staff, want to give a huge thanks to the city and the fans [for making] it a tremendous atmosphere for all of us. I know there are a lot of players on the New York team who are extremely envious of what we have here. Big thank you.

—*Kasey Keller*

At the conclusion of the match, the team began one of many new traditions by walking the field's perimeter to applaud the fans before gathering at the south end of the stadium to take a bow for the Emerald City Supporter Group (ECS).

Throughout the season, Sounders FC urged its supporters to give the club their *full 90* with the return guarantee that the team would bring a physical and mental commitment to winning each time it stepped on the pitch. The fans made good on their half of the bargain by setting a new MLS season attendance record—many going so far as to stand the entire match in support of their club. And true to its word, Sounders FC delivered the personnel and brand of play required to hoist a U.S. Open Cup Championship trophy and earn an MLS Cup playoff berth, rare feats for an expansion team. On the defensive side of the ball, Sounders FC engaged in physical and mental clashes with a grit described by soccer players as being "stuck in." Through hard challenges and physical play across all 11 positions, the team issued a clear statement to its opponents and fans that it was there to give its *full 90*.

GIVING THEIR FULL 90

Midfielder Osvaldo Alonso elevates against Toronto FC's Jim Brennan in a 0-0 draw (August 29, 2009).

Cuban international Alonso was an unknown quantity to Sounders fans, having joined the team prior to its MLS debut, but it didn't take long before he endeared himself to fans with his tenacious and consistent play in the heart of the Sounders' formation.

Practice makes perfect. Goalkeeper Kasey Keller practices punching the ball in warm-ups and then skillfully putting it into action during a 3-3 draw with D.C. United (June 17, 2009).

RIGHT: The Sounders FC team captain anchored the team's defense with an impressive 10 shutouts in his 12 wins during the season.

We've got guys that are willing to work extremely hard, to put their body on the line and do what needs to be done to keep the other team off the board, and I think if we continue with that mentality all year we've got a very good shot at having a very good season.

—*Kasey Keller*

Central defender Jhon Kennedy Hurtado holds his ground against the Chicago Fire's Patrick Nyarko in a 0-0 draw (July 25, 2009).

Defender Patrick Ianni wins a header against the San Jose Earthquakes' Ryan Johnson in a 2-1 win (June 13, 2009).

Jamaican national team and Sounders FC central defender Tyrone Marshall clears a ball against Chivas USA in a 0-0 draw (September 19, 2009).

Defender Zach Scott beats a New England
Revolution player to the ball in a 0-1 loss
(August 20, 2009).

Defender Nathan Sturgis holds off U.S. national team and LA Galaxy forward Landon Donovan to win a header in a 1-1 draw (May 10, 2009).

It was an absolute pleasure to wear the Sounders colors this year. I thoroughly enjoyed my teammates and the fan support was epic. There is no better place to play.

—*James Riley*

Sounders FC selected defender James Riley in the 2008 Expansion Draft from the San Jose Earthquakes. James earned a starting spot with the team and the respect of the supporters with his fiery personality and durability. Riley clocked 2,334 minutes on the pitch during the regular season, a total that he and Jhon Kennedy Hurtado shared for second on the team. Kasey Keller led the team with 2,549 minutes played.

Osvaldo Alonso (left) and Brad Evans (right) played center midfield together in most matches. The pair illustrated that a match is often won in the spine of the field with high energy and physical play.

Signed by the club in early July 2009, Costa Rican national team defender Leo Gonzales made his first appearance on August 5, 2009, against FC Barcelona in an international friendly. From that point on, he claimed the left fullback position by fighting for possessions and then spurring the team's offense.

Leo can play left back, play center back in a pinch, and he can also play wide and run the whole line for us. He is an attacking left fullback with good size and athleticism.

—*Head coach Sigi Schmid*

Midfielder Sebastien Le Toux closely marks New England Revolution's Kevin Alston in a 0-1 loss (August 20, 2009).

LEFT: Defender Tyson Wahl overpowers D.C. United forward Ange N'Silu in a 3-3 draw (June 17, 2009).

A tenacious midfielder, Freddie Ljungberg is constantly stuck in. Here he outmuscles a Columbus Crew opponent in a 1-1 draw (May 30, 2009).

In order to score goals, a soccer team must move the ball up the pitch. Match after match in 2009, Sounders FC showcased its ability to do just that with an impressive array of offensive weapons. By incorporating the entire team into the offense, the Sounders worked the ball to each other and exposed holes in their opponent's defense. Each position player had a role—outside backs and midfielders flew forward to cross the ball into the box, center midfielders pinned back their ears and carved through the opposition, strikers used their size and speed to create scoring opportunities, and central defenders applied their heading prowess to connect on corner kicks. Improvements in 2010 and beyond will focus on refining the offense to match an already stellar defense, and if what we glimpsed in 2009 continues to evolve, Sounders FC could soon be lifting its first MLS Cup.

MANY MOVING PARTS

Forward Fredy Montero flies high to head the ball against the San Jose Earthquakes in a 2-0 win (April 25, 2009).

Colombian international Montero burst onto the MLS scene with two goals and an assist in the Sounders FC's MLS debut. Montero's and his fellow players' accomplishments were intertwined as he scored the first-ever goal for the club in its first win, which netted him MLS Goal of the Week honors and MLS Player of the Month for March.

Fans appreciated right defender James Riley's offensive runs, which broke down the defense of Sounders FC opponents.

Defender Leonardo Gonzalez outmaneuvers New England Revolution's Kevin Alston in a 0-1 loss (August 20, 2009).

The speedster, Steve Zakuani, settled into the left-midfield position as the season progressed.

Roger's a hard-working forward; always trying to find spaces.

—*Head coach Sigi Schmid*

Fan favorite and former Sounders USL-1 player Roger Levesque made the most of his minutes in 2009, bringing high energy and clinical finishes. Levesque appeared in twenty-one matches and started five while tallying four goals and five assists.

Fredy Montero shows just how hard he is to defend by cutting through two D.C. United players in a 3-3 draw (June 17, 2009).

> Vagenas in midfield is a very good organizer. . . . He's one of those guys who, through his organization, makes the guy next to him a little bit better.
>
> —*Head coach Sigi Schmid*

Midfielder Sebastien Le Toux fires off a shot in a 0-0 draw with Toronto FC (August 29, 2009).

CENTER: MLS veteran midfielder Peter Vagenas uncorks a rocket shot in a 1-1 draw with the Columbus Crew (May 30, 2009).

LEFT: Gambian national team player and MLS rookie Sanna Nyassi appeared in twenty matches and started seven in 2009. Nyassi's blazing speed allows him to get behind opposing defenses (May 10, 2009).

OPPOSITE: Sounders FC named Tyrone Marshall its defender of the year in 2009. Here, Marshall comes forward on a corner kick to face off against the 2009 MLS Keeper of the Year, Chivas USA's Zach Thornton. The match finished in a scoreless draw (September 19, 2009).

Forward Nate Jaqua played the role of target man to perfection in 2009, using his 6'4" frame to hold off defenders or head the ball on to his teammates.

Midfielder Brad Evans throws the ball in during a 0-1 loss to the Kansas City Wizards (April 11, 2009).

. . . the fans have been amazing and have been very welcoming to me to come here. It's over anything I have imagined.

—*Freddie Ljungberg*

Swedish International, former English Premier League player, and current Sounders FC midfielder Freddie Ljungberg had a huge impact on the league in his first season. Ljungberg scored two goals and had nine assists in all 2009 competitions, pausing at the mid-point to captain the MLS All Star Team.

Midfielder Brad Evans knows what it takes to win an MLS Cup, having won it with the Columbus Crew in 2008. As a member of Sounders FC, Evans earned a national team call-up and played in the 2009 CONCACAF Gold Cup for the United States, which included an appearance at Seattle's Qwest Field in a 4-0 win over Grenada on July 4.

It's just an honor, to be honest. You play as good as you can for your club to get recognized by your country.

—*Brad Evans*

Sounders FC selected midfielder Stephen King from the Chicago Fire in the 2008 MLS Expansion Draft. Here, he leaps to avoid goalkeeper Donovan Ricketts in a 1-1 draw with the LA Galaxy (May 10, 2009).

Forward Fredy Montero takes flight to avoid a slide tackle from a Houston Dynamo defender.

To celebrate a goal is to appreciate the intricacies of its creation. Goals are magical occasions envisioned by club management, crafted by coaching staffs, forged in training by players, and willed into existence by team supporters before they finally hit the back of the net on match day. These infrequent events are brought about by a combination of skill, speed, strength, and strategy, but frustratingly remain so elusive. While just one player claims the cherished statistic, each and every goal can be attributed to the efforts of the entire club.

GOAL CELEBRATIONS

Steve Zakuani reacts to his first assist in the MLS—a superb cross to Nate Jaqua in a 2-0 win over Real Salt Lake (March 28, 2009).

Even though we speak different languages, at least we are making ourselves understood now. Two intelligent guys can always understand each other. That makes things easier. Obviously this is good for the team. And we are scoring the goals.

—*Fredy Montero*

Fredy Montero tackles Nate Jaqua after assisting his goal in a 2-1 win over FC Dallas (October 24, 2009).

Together the Sounders forward tandem scored more than half of the team's 2009 regular season goals—Montero led the team by netting twelve, while Jaqua followed with nine.

Early on, the language barrier slowed the pair's progress and chemistry, but they worked hard to overcome it. The breakthrough came on June 28 in a 3-0 win over the Colorado Rapids—the two combined on all three goals.

Bound by a common language, the "Three Amigos" (Osvaldo Alonso, Fredy Montero, and Jhon Kennedy Hurtado) embrace following a goal in a 3-3 draw with D.C. United (June 17, 2009).

Fredy Montero celebrates his ninth goal of the season in a 2-1 win over the Houston Dynamo (July 11, 2009).

James Riley roars his approval at Nate Jaqua's goal in a 1-1 draw with the Columbus Crew (May 30, 2009).

If you would have told me at the beginning of the game that we would have won the game on a bicycle kick, and I had to pick one of my players that was going to score the bicycle kick, I think (Patrick) Ianni would have been number nine.

—*Assistant coach Brian Schmetzer*

Patrick Ianni celebrates a 2-1 win over the Houston Dynamo—his spectacular bicycle kick goal earned him MLS Goal of the Week honors (July 11, 2009).

Brad Evans pumps his fists to celebrate one of the team's three goals in a 3-0 win over the Colorado Rapids (June 28, 2009).

For every goal celebration, there is contrasting dejection. Colorado Rapids goalkeeper Matt Pickens walks away as the Sounders celebrate Fredy Montero's goal in a 3-0 win on the day (June 28, 2009).

Brad Evans feels the love after scoring his first Sounders goal, contributing to a 3-0 win over the New York Red Bulls (March 19, 2009).

He's a young guy. Of course he's from Arsenal, he's from London. We talk a bit. I might try to talk to him about some things he can do better, and try to advise him. He's a very good player.

—*Freddie Ljungberg*

Freddie Ljungberg celebrates with Steve Zakuani after Ljungberg scores his second goal of the season in a 2-1 win over the San Jose Earthquakes (June 13, 2009).

Ljungberg shares a special connection with Zakuani, whom the Sounders selected as the first overall pick in the 2009 MLS SuperDraft. Ljungberg, now 32, appeared in 328 matches for England's Arsenal Football Club from 1998 to 2007, scoring 72 goals, while Zakuani, now 22, played with the Arsenal youth team until age 14 (1997 to 2002).

By pairing the two players in their lineup, the team members hope that a bit of Ljungberg's experience will wear off on the talented rookie.

Brad Evans congratulates Steve Zakuani on scoring the first goal of his MLS career in a 2-0 win over the San Jose Earthquakes (April 25, 2009).

LEFT: Seattle Sounders FC fans are on hand to celebrate every home goal for their club. In 2009, Sounders FC set a new MLS season record for attendance with an average of 30,897.

There's been a lot of good coaches in this league, and to have won more games than any of them fills me with a lot of humbleness—and also a lot of honor and pride to know that I was able to accomplish that.

—Head coach Sigi Schmid

Sounders FC majority owner Joe Roth presents Sigi Schmid with a plaque after the Sounders' 2-1 win over FC Dallas on October 24, 2009. Schmid's 125th win is the most of any MLS coach in history, and is true cause for celebration. Schmid bested former MLS coach Bob Bradley's record total of 124.

During the 2009 MLS regular season, Sounders FC scored 38 goals over the span of 30 matches. The team spread the scoring across 11 different players—defenders, midfielders, and forwards alike. Each goal represents a true team accomplishment.

Soccer players on all levels compete to win, and it's no different for the athletes in MLS. A player's on-field intensity is fueled by his culture, personality, and motivations. Imagine your favorite Sounder hustling to uphold his reputation, earning a spot on his country's national team, or breaking into the starting lineup, and you will recognize a bit of yourself in him. Perhaps that's why we all love to see the blood boil and watch our favorite player deliver or take exception to a hard foul—it's cathartic. Sounders FC players had their heated moments in 2009, and in those moments we experienced their passion for the game, their devotion to their teammates, and their resilience in the face of adversity.

HEAT OF BATTLE

Freddie Ljungberg steps into the fray to make his point, following an exchange that left LA Galaxy player Mike Magee on the turf and James Riley with a red card. Sounders FC drew 1-1 with the Galaxy on this Mother's Day match to remember (May 10, 2009).

Sounders FC selected forward Nate Jaqua in the 2008 Expansion Draft from the Houston Dynamo. In two different matches, the "Sounder Solider" suffered bleeding head wounds in matches against his former club. The iconic image of Jaqua in a head wrap inspired Halloween costumes and supporters' flags.

Nate seems to get wrapped up every time we play them. As I said, it's part of it.

—*Head coach Sigi Schmid*

Sounders FC players feel the heat and intensity of their opponents as well. Fans will never forget the fiery D.C. United goalkeeper Josh Wicks for his red card stomp of Fredy Montero in the U.S. Open Cup Championship match.

Kansas City Wizards' goalkeeper Kevin Hartman and defender Jimmy Conrad take Nate Jaqua to task for colliding with Hartman (April 11, 2009).

OPPOSITE: Defenders Jhon Kennedy Hurtado and Patrick Ianni mix it up with Houston Dynamo players during the team's first-leg match of the MLS playoffs. Six yellow cards were issued in an epic battle ending in a 0-0 draw (October 29, 2009).

Houston Dynamo goalkeeper Pat Onstad collects a yellow card for giving Fredy Montero (right) a chest bump that sent the forward sprawling to the ground. Montero also received a yellow card for the altercation (October 29, 2009).

Patrick Ianni howls after missing a shot on goal in a 0-1 loss to the New England Revolution (August 20, 2009).

LEFT: Patrick Ianni restrains Freddie Ljungberg during a 0-0 draw with the Chicago Fire (July 25, 2009).

Casualties of War:

A Toronto FC player leaves the field injured during a matchup with the Sounders FC (August 28, 2009).

LEFT: Tyrone Marshall is carried off on a stretcher during a Sounders FC versus San Jose Earthquakes match (June 13, 2009).

OPPOSITE: Head coach Sigi Schmid reacts to something that he doesn't appreciate in a 0-0 draw with Toronto FC (August 29, 2009).

Chivas USA defender Marcelo Saragosa collects a red card ejection for cleating Fredy Montero (September 19, 2009). Later, the MLS Disciplinary Committee piled on a two-match suspension and a $500 fine to Saragosa for the foul.

. . . when I realized what was going on, I already felt the boot on my face. And it hurt. . . . In this game, it was definitely the hardest foul. In other situations, like set pieces, you have the opportunity to protect your face. But in this one I really didn't have any opportunity, and it just came like that.

—*Fredy Montero*

Emotions escalate in the 68th minute when Sounders FC faced off against Toronto FC. The vigilant Riley and Ljungberg came to the rescue of their teammate Jhon Kennedy Hurtado (August 29, 2009).

There had already been a couple occurrences where it appeared they pushed our guys into the boards. That wasn't dealt with, so it was probably a push from us and De Rosario reacted. The rest was what you saw on the field.

—*Head coach Sigi Schmid*

Tempers can rise even in a friendly match. Brazil International and Barcelona FC defender Dani Alves takes exception to a Freddie Ljungberg challenge in Barca's 0-4 win (August 5, 2009).

Sportsmanship quells the battle. Mexico International and Chicago Fire designated player Cuauhtémoc Blanco is one of the fiercest competitors in the MLS. Here he is helped to his feet by the silent-yet-steely Jhon Kennedy Hurtado.

The Lamar Hunt U.S. Open Cup tournament dates back to 1914. The contest is open to all United States Soccer Federation—affiliated teams, ranging from adult clubs to MLS professional franchises. Since its inception in 1996, MLS has dominated the competition, winning 12 cups over the past 13 years. Remarkably, the Chicago Fire won the cup as an MLS expansion team in 1998, and Sounders FC aspired to second that statistic in 2009. That lofty goal gave the newly formed team an opportunity to show its fans, the league, and itself that it was championship material. Over the course of four months, Seattle played through five elimination matches, setting the stage for the championship match in the nation's capital against the defending Cup champions, D.C. United. After the team's thrilling win in D.C. on September 2, the 2009 U.S. Open Cup Champion Sounders FC touched down at Boeing Field to an enthusiastic welcome by hundreds of supporters. A special Cup run had reached a magical conclusion.

U.S. OPEN CUP CHAMPIONS

Sounders FC huddle before the opening match versus Real Salt Lake (April 28, 2009). The Sounders won handily, 4-1, but despite the thrashing, Real Salt Lake would be back in Seattle to win the MLS Cup just five months later.

The Starfire Sports Stadium in Tukwila, Washington, was the scene for four of the team's six Open Cup matches in 2009. A familiar and intimate venue for fans and players of the USL-1 Sounders, the stadium packs in 4,000-plus supporters to cheer their team.

The crowd is close and . . . pro-Seattle, which gives us a good advantage and certainly helps our team.

—*Head coach Sigi Schmid*

Forward Roger Levesque played in all six Open Cup matches, scoring two goals and providing three assists.

Open Cup play provides opportunities for second-team players to make their mark. Backup goalkeeper Chris Eylander warms up for his second start of the season. Kasey Keller's backup and former USL-1 Sounder saw action in two matches in 2009.

Former USL-1 Sounders defender Taylor Graham suffered several injuries in 2009, but he was fit and active on the backline in this match (April 28, 2009). While injured, Graham focused his time on the local community, and he earned the club's Humanitarian of the Year award.

Midfielder Sanna Nyassi soars after scoring in the team's 4-1 win over Real Salt Lake (April 28, 2009).

Sounders FC and Colorado Rapids players march out for their play-in match. Sounders FC advanced to the third round of the Open Cup with a 1-0 win (May 26, 2009).

Sounders FC selected defender/midfielder Nathan Sturgis from Real Salt Lake in the 2008 Expansion Draft. Sturgis is a two-year MLS veteran who started all 15 matches in his rookie season with the LA Galaxy.

Defender Evan Brown marks up former
USL-1 Sounder Ciaran O'Brien (May 26,
2009). Selected by Sounders FC with
the 16th overall pick in the 2009 MLS
SuperDraft, Brown played in two Open Cup
matches and saw time in both international
friendlies.

A former University of Washington standout and Pac-10 Player of the Year, forward Kevin Forrest played nine matches for the USL-1 Sounders in 2008 before Sounders FC signed him to its development squad.

Forrest played in just one match for the Sounders FC. In the Open Cup match versus Colorado Rapids, he headed home what was to be his only shot on goal for the club—a match winner in the 62nd minute. Sounders FC waived Forrest from the team in June, but he went on to play for the USL-1 Portland Timbers for the remainder of 2009.

CENTER: Kevin Forrest celebrates his game-winning goal and inspires a supporter banner the following week at Qwest Field.

After winning its third-round match against the Portland Timbers in Oregon, Sounders FC returned to Starfire Sports Stadium for a quarterfinal match versus the Kansas City Wizards. Sounders FC advanced to the semifinal round with a 1-0 win (August 7, 2009).

Defender Patrick Ianni pushes the ball up
the pitch (August 7, 2009).

Midfielder Sanna Nyassi hustles to win a
50/50 ball (August 7, 2009).

In a pivotal moment late in the match, Kansas City Wizards goalkeeper Kevin Hartman trips up Fredy Montero in the 89th minute, resulting in a penalty-kick opportunity for Sounders FC (August 7, 2009).

Sebastien Le Toux, "Mr. Open Cup," finishes the penalty kick awarded on the Montero foul and is subsequently mobbed by his teammates.

Of course there is always pressure on you. I knew I had [to] score. I was confident and lucky the keeper did not stop it.

—*Sebastien Le Toux*

Ten disciplinary cards were issued to the two teams during the match, and forward Nate Jaqua wound up with the first of his two head bandages of the season (August 28, 2009).

The ever-dependable James Riley played in all six of the Sounders' Open Cup matches (August 28, 2009).

In the 89th minute, Nate Jaqua scores the equalizing goal on an assist from Le Toux to Levesque. Stephen King would score five minutes later in extra time to advance the Sounders FC to the U.S. Open Cup Championship versus D.C. United (September 2, 2009).

This is the pot of gold at the end of the rainbow for the Open Cup. We are happy we won the tournament, but the big prize is the Champions League.

—*Sounders FC owner and general manager Adrian Hanauer*

After its 2-1 win in Washington, D.C., versus D.C. United, the club returned to Seattle, where it was presented with the Lamar Hunt U.S. Open Cup trophy before the evening's match versus Chivas USA (September 19, 2009).

Sounders FC earned one of the four U.S. slots in the 2010–11 CONCACAF Champions League by virtue of its USOC Final victory.

In recognition of Seattle's rich soccer heritage, the Sounders FC established a tradition in its inaugural season to publicly honor key members of the community. Before each home match, in conjunction with flags and much fanfare, the club bestows the prestigious Golden Scarf upon a noteworthy individual, which the recipient stretches overhead—mirrored by an impressive array of scarf-bearing fans in the stands. The symbolic scarf gives a nod to the European game, but the Golden Scarf is decidedly American. In a variation of the Seattle Seahawks' ritual of allowing community members to raise the "12" flag on game day, the honorees are selected for their connection to the sport or for their impact in the region. The Golden Scarf ceremony signals the official start of the on-field festivities, but more important, it unifies the supporters as they celebrate the people that enrich their city and team.

THE GOLDEN SCARF

A procession of colorful flags, along with the sounds of the Golden Scarf anthem, signals the start of a Sounders FC match day.

Before each home game, match-day staff usher the Golden Scarf recipient and the ceremonial presenter to the platform. The Golden Scarf is transported in a wooden case lined with Sounders FC colors and neon lights.

I felt pretty emotional down on the field before the game kicked off. That was very special—one of the most special experiences in my entire career, quite frankly.

—*Don Garber, MLS commissioner*

Don Garber—March 19, 2009 vs. New York Red Bulls

Sounders FC owner and general manager Adrian Hanauer unveils the Golden Scarf for presentation by Governor Gregoire to Commissioner Garber. Sounders FC CEO Tod Leiweke (opposite; top far left), majority owner Joe Roth (opposite; top far right), and owner Drew Carey (above; far right) look on.

LEFT: In May 2008, the Sounders FC inked a multiyear sponsorship with Microsoft and Xbox 360. Robbie Bach is president of Microsoft's Entertainment and Devices division, which produces the Xbox 360.

RIGHT: Jimmy Gabriel—March 28, 2009 vs. Real Salt Lake

The Scottish-born Gabriel played extensively with England's Everton FC before moving to the United States in 1974 to join the NASL Seattle Sounders. Gabriel scored the Sounders' first goal in the newly built Kingdome and went on to coach the team from 1977 to 1979.

All of our employees and customers are soccer fans, so this is a great opportunity in a local way to connect with that audience.

—*Robbie Bach*

Jimmy McAlister—April 24, 2009 vs. San
Jose Earthquakes

A Seattle native, McAlister earned NASL
Rookie of the Year honors with the
Sounders in 1977.

Meredith Teague—May 10, 2009 vs.
LA Galaxy

A member of the Seattle Pacific University
women's soccer team, Teague collected a
Golden Scarf to go with her NCAA Division
II Women's national championship title and
NCAA Division II National Player of the
Year honors.

To feel the energy is so exciting. It really got me excited for the start of our season.

—*Jim Mora*

Jim Mora—May 30, 2009 vs. Columbus Crew

Sigi Schmid's Qwest Field coaching counterpart, Jim Mora, received the Golden Scarf a few months before his Seattle Seahawks began to share Qwest Field with the Sounders FC during the 2009 season. In early 2008, the Seattle Seahawks signed Mora as head coach effective for 2009.

Seattle Storm—June 17, 2009 vs. D.C. United

Sue Bird (front) and Swin Cash raised Golden Scarves on behalf of their entire basketball team. The Seattle Storm play in the Women's National Basketball Association (WNBA).

Fred Mendoza—June 30, 2009 vs. San Jose Earthquakes

Scarf recipient Mendoza is a member of the Washington State Public Stadium Authority (PSA), which was voted into existence by statewide referendum on June 17, 1997. The PSA went on to ensure that Qwest Field was built to host both American football and soccer.

We kept saying it's never a question of if, it's a question of when MLS will come . . . timing is everything, and this ownership group has done it right . . .[the group] made this dream everything that all of us in the beginning wanted it to be and expected it to be, and Seattle deserves no less.

—*Fred Mendoza*

Lorenzo Romar—June 28, 2009 vs.
Colorado Rapids

University of Washington men's basketball
coach Lorenzo Romar was named the
2008 Pacific 10 Conference Coach of
the Year after leading the Huskies to the
conference title.

Doug Andreassen—July 11, 2009 vs.
Houston Dynamo

Washington State Youth Soccer president
Andreassen oversees statewide soccer
for 130,000 kids ages 5 to 19. The
organization is one of four Sounders FC
charity partners.

Dale Chihuly—July 18, 2009 vs. Chelsea FC

Tacoma native and University of Washington graduate Chihuly is a well-known glass sculptor. Together with the Sounders FC, he designed the Emerald Spire for presentation to the team's 2009 friendly opponents, Chelsea FC and Barcelona FC.

It was a lot of fun to design and make the commemorative artwork for the Sounders FC and the visiting international teams.

—*Dale Chihuly*

Mike Ryan—July 25, 2009 vs. Chicago Fire

This Irishman has been an integral part of the local soccer community since he arrived in 1962. Ryan served as the first president of both the Washington state youth and women's associations and coached, among others, the University of Washington men's and U.S. women's national teams.

Bill Russell—August 5, 2009 vs. FC Barcelona

Sounders FC scarved this 11-time NBA champion and Boston Celtic before its friendly with the 2008 European champs, FC Barcelona. From 1973 to 1977, Russell coached the Seattle SuperSonics, leading them to the first playoffs in team history. He now calls Seattle his home.

John Nordstrom—August 20, 2009 vs.
New England Revolution

The son of the department store's founder,
Nordstrom was a member of the NASL
Seattle Sounders ownership group in
1974 and the original owner of the Seattle
Seahawks in 1976.

Michelle Akers—August 29, 2009 vs.
Toronto FC

A member of the 1999 United States
World Cup champion women's team and
the National Soccer Hall of Fame, Akers—
with her teammates—raised the sport's
popularity in America. After receiving
the Golden Scarf, Akers spoke of her
connection to Seattle's new soccer team.

There's a love affair going on between the old Sounders fans and new Sounders fans . . . the sky's the limit for this club.

—*Alan Hinton*

Alan Hinton—September 19, 2009 vs. Chivas USA

Sounders FC owner and general manager Adrian Hanauer presents a Golden Scarf to Hinton, a former NASL Sounders coach from 1980 to 1982. In 1980, Hinton's team finished 25-7, tallying the best season record in NASL history. On a day when the club honored all the former NASL Sounders in a pre-game ceremony, the season ticket holders voted for Hinton to receive the scarf.

It was an amazing night, a once-in-a-lifetime experience. I am truly humbled to have received a Golden Scarf on behalf of the fans that I represent as a Sounders FC Alliance Council member.

—*Greg Roth (photo center)*

Sounders FC Alliance Council—October 24, 2009 vs. FC Dallas

Several 2009 Sounders FC Alliance Council members raise their Golden Scarves. Shown left to right: Robby Branom, Mark Inderhees, Greg Mockos, Greg Roth, Kevin Zelko, and Iain Starr. (Council members not shown: Dave Clark, Leann Johnson, Nick Ewing, Rachel Molloy, and Tom Challinor.)

The Seattle Sounders FC's official members association (i.e., Alliance) provides the means for fans to participate in the decision-making process of the team.

Chris Henderson—October 29, 2009 vs. Houston Dynamo

On the night of the franchise's first playoff match, Adrian Hanauer scarves former U.S. Men's national team and MLS veteran Chris Henderson. Henderson hails from Edmonds, Washington, and returned to the area to become the Sounders FC technical director.

American soccer fans turned their eyes to Seattle several times in 2009, first for the team's thrilling debut on March 19, 2009, and again as the city hosted 2005–06 English Premier League champion Chelsea FC and 2008–09 Spanish La Liga and FIFA European champions Barcelona FC in international friendly matches. The European soccer giants kicked Seattle's tires and took the Sounders FC on a test drive, liking what they saw, and then telling the world. The city played host a third time for the MLS Cup on November 22, 2009. By the time Real Salt Lake lifted the Cup in celebration, many acknowledged Seattle's role in furthering American soccer. To cap a storybook season, the Sounders FC became champions themselves with a U.S. Open Cup title and a plan to continue that success for many years to come.

SEATTLE: HOST TO CHAMPIONS

Widely considered the best central defender in the sport, England national team captain John Terry tackles Nate Jaqua to set the tone early in a friendly match on July 18, 2009. A crowd of 65,289 watched as England's Chelsea FC overcame Sounders FC 0-2.

Defender James Riley matches up with French national team and Chelsea FC striker Nicolas Anelka.

Defender Tyson Wahl played in 18 games across all team competitions in 2009, including 45 minutes versus Chelsea FC.

Defender Jhon Kennedy Hurtado chases defender Ashley Cole. Cole plays for both the England national team and Chelsea FC.

Midfielder Steve Zakuani avoids Chelsea FC and Brazilian International defender Juliano Belletti.

Chelsea FC fans enjoyed the club's four-city American tour in summer 2009. The Blues played in Seattle (versus Sounders FC), Pasadena (versus Inter Milan), Baltimore (versus AC Milan), and Arlington (versus Club America).

Midfielder Osvaldo Alonso defends Daniel Sturridge. The Sounders FC friendly was also young Sturridge's Chelsea FC debut—he collected a goal and an assist on the day.

Forward Fredy Montero entered the Chelsea friendly as the MLS leading scorer amid rumors of his potential transfer to a European club. Here, he outmaneuvers Frank Lampard, who was recently named the English Premier League's Player of the Decade based on statistics.

Petr Cech, Czech Republic national team and Chelsea FC goalkeeper, covers the ball while forward Nate Jaqua and Chelsea FC defender Alex fly over him in tandem.

Midfielder Sebastien Le Toux pushes the ball down the flank against Portuguese national team player and Chelsea FC defender Ricardo Carvalho.

Five or six years ago the stadium was not full when we came to the U.S. It looks like soccer became more popular and closed the gap on the big sports, like football and baseball.

—*Michael Ballack*

German national team captain and Chelsea midfielder Michael Ballack signs autographs following the match.

In 2009, FC Barcelona was champion six times over. The club won the Spanish League, FIFA Club World Cup, European Super Cup, Spanish Cup, Spanish Super Cup, and the biggest prize of all, the UEFA Champions League.

Spain's FC Barcelona brings intensity to all its matches, and it was no different for its 0-4 friendly match victory over Sounders FC on August 5, 2009 before the largest crowd in Qwest Field history—66,848.

Defender Leonardo Gonzalez made his Sounders FC debut against FC Barcelona and was immediately entrusted with the Herculean task of facing off against Argentine national team forward Lionel Messi.

Gonzalez impressed Sounders FC fans with a solid performance against the 2009 FIFA World Player of the Year.

FC Barcelona's Lionel Messi (#10)
prepares to strike a free kick.

They have great technical ability and they keep the ball really well. It was just great for the fans to come and see the game, and enjoy it.

—Freddie Ljungberg

Brazilian national team and FC Barcelona right back Dani Alves slides through Sounders FC speedster Steve Zakuani.

BELOW: In a battle of the midfield, Freddie Ljungberg holds off Spanish national team and FC Barcelona midfielder Xavier Hernandez Creus (aka Xavi).

Forward Roger Levesque matches up with
FC Barcelona defender Gerard Piqué.

Defenders Patrick Ianni (front) and Taylor
Graham pair up in the center defense
to mark FC Barcelona forward Pedro
Rodríguez Ledesma.

Xavi flicks a clever ball over forward Fredy Montero's head. The Barcelona midfielder assisted Lionel Messi on the second goal in the match.

The Xbox Pitch at Qwest Field was the site of the November 22, 2009, MLS Cup match—a contest featuring Real Salt Lake captain Kyle Beckerman and LA Galaxy star David Beckham.

46,011 fans were on hand to watch Real Salt Lake best the LA Galaxy 5-4 on penalty kicks to become the 2009 MLS Champions.

Real Salt Lake backup keeper Chris Seitz wouldn't see action in the MLS Cup, but he did during the Cup week festivities at Seattle's Pike Place Market.

Real Salt Lake fans got a taste of the Sounders FC fan experience during the MLS Cup March to the Match from Occidental Park in Seattle.

Sounders FC supporter "Mr. Mohawk" changes his look for the MLS Cup event.

Sounders FC players James Riley (left)
and Tyrone Marshall were spectators in
their home stadium.

Sounders FC defender Leo Gonzalez
enjoys the pre-match ceremony. The club
honored the 2009 Sounders FC players
who fell short of making it to the MLS Cup
match, but had a fantastic debut season
nonetheless.

The Sounders FC match-day staff parades the MLS Cup Championship trophy onto the pitch in lieu of their usual Golden Scarf case.

Sounders FC fans in attendance witness one of the most recognizable figures in the sport, David Beckham, in action. Beckham missed the club's regular season match at Qwest Field on May 10, 2009. The English superstar spent the first half of the MLS season in Italy on loan to AC Milan.

Real Salt Lake forwards Robbie Findley (left) and Yura Movsisyan celebrate Findley's match-equalizing goal in the 64th minute.

Real Salt Lake goalkeeper Nick Rimando rushes to congratulate teammate Robbie Russell after Russell netted his shoot-out penalty kick to win the MLS Cup.

LA Galaxy forward Landon Donovan consoles teammate Edson Buddle after the match. Both Donovan and Buddle missed their penalty kick opportunities.

Kyle Beckerman soars into a pile of jubilant teammates.

The launch of the Sounders will go down as one of the key moments in the history of this sport in this country.

—MLS commissioner Don Garber

The 2009 MLS Cup Champion Real Salt Lake celebrates becoming the 14th MLS season title-holder. The moment concluded a magical 2009 MLS season, which began and ended at Qwest Field in Seattle.

Seattle Sounders FC recognizes the critical role that supporters play in the success of the organization. At the outset, it was clear that the club was committed to building a new tradition in partnership with the city. Seattleites saw it first in the new owners' willingness to compromise on the team name, and then later as they unveiled a membership association with the power to retain or retire the club's general manager every four years. Clearly democracy was always in the blueprint, as two of the three options proposed by the club in the "name the team" vote referenced the concept—Seattle Alliance and Seattle Republic. The members association now bears the name Alliance and through it, the club has struck a chord with supporters. Seattle Sounders FC is a team of the supporters, by the supporters, for the supporters, and loves its new republic.

THE SUPPORTERS

Sounders Supporters' Song
Sounders 'Til I Die

I'm Sounders 'til I die
I'm Sounders 'til I die
I know I am, I'm sure I am
I'm Sounders 'til I die

Sections 121 to 123 in the south end of Qwest Field are home to the Emerald City Supporters (ECS). ECS members are at the core of the club, loyal to the last, and indifferent to the number of sellouts or season tickets sold. They are and always will be Sounders 'til they die.

Expressive Sounders FC fans cover themselves in rave green and blue to support their club.

Scarves up, Seattle! Fans hold their scarves aloft in support of their club.

Sounders FC season ticket holders received a green "2009 Season Ticket Holder Inaugural Season Scarf" along with their printed tickets.

A note in the Sounders FC season ticket package informed fans that the enclosed scarf was their ticket to the opening match. Fans—of course—wore them to every match, even in the heat of July.

A Sounders FC fan pays tribute to the late King of Pop, Michael Jackson, during a match against Colorado Rapids (June 28, 2009).

In the ninth minute of the Sounders FC versus Dallas FC match on October 24, 2009, fans stand and hold signs bearing the number 9 in support of U.S. Men's National Team player Charlie Davies. Davies was involved in a serious car accident 10 days earlier that threatened his professional playing career.

The recognizable Sounders FC supporter "Mr. Mohawk" shares the match-day experience with a next-gen supporter.

A young club supporter sports a rave green faux-hawk.

Midfielder Freddie Ljungberg talks with a young fan after the team's June 13, 2009, match versus San Jose Earthquakes.

Young autograph seekers hope to capture the attention of their favorite Sounders FC players.

Sebastien Le Toux signs a fan's jersey through the railing at Qwest Field. Le Toux and defender James Riley (right) were fan favorites, both for their play on the pitch, and for their devotion to signing each and every autograph request after home matches.

A sizeable group of traveling Chicago Fire fans attends their team's road match versus Sounders FC at Qwest Field (July 25, 2009).

OPPOSITE: Sounders FC supporters enjoy the match-day festivities.

The north and south ends of Qwest Field are home to the various supporter groups of Seattle Sounders FC. On display in their sections are colorful and inventive *tifo*, which is short for the Italian word *tifoso*, meaning supporter. It's used as a general term to describe flags, banners, confetti, balloons, paper rolls, smoke, flares, scarves, and any display that supports one's club.

Early on in the season, Keith Hodo from Emerald City Supporters and I began what has now become the famous Seeeeeaaaaatllle . . . Soooooouunnnders chant lobbed back and forth between the south and north ends of Qwest. We texted back and forth to start it up in the beginning, but now the entire stadium knows what to do—it's really caught on.

—*Joe Thomas, North End Supporters co-founder and president*

An Emerald City Supporter strikes an iconic pose.

It's been beyond anybody's wildest dreams. . . . The fans continue to come out, game after game. The support that we've gotten from the city, the love that [the fans] have showered upon our team and the organization . . . hopefully we've returned it to them as well. We just want this to continue. I don't want to wake up if this is a dream.

—*Head coach Sigi Schmid*

Sounders FC players take a bow to the fans in appreciation for their support.

SEATTLE
SOUNDERS FC

SEATTLE SOUNDERS

TIME LINE (1974–2009)

1997: Voters approve a statewide referendum for a new stadium and event center on June 17, resulting in the formation of the Washington State Public Stadium Authority to oversee the public's interest in the facility. The expectation was that the stadium would be designed as a multipurpose venue for both football and soccer.

2002: Seahawks Stadium opens on July 28. The first sporting event held is a USL Division 1 Seattle Sounders match versus Vancouver Whitecaps—a match that the Sounders won 4-1 in front of 25,515 fans. In 2004, the stadium was renamed Qwest Field.

| 1974 | 1983 | 1994 | 1997 | 2002 | 2007 | 2008 |

1974–1983: The Seattle Sounders play in the North American Soccer League (NASL). The club played in both Memorial Stadium and the Kingdome in Seattle. Highlights include two Western Division Championships (1980, 1982) and a National Conference Championship (1977).

1994–2008: The Seattle Sounders play in the American Professional Soccer League (APSL) and later in the United Soccer League (USL) First Division. The club played in numerous venues including Memorial Stadium, Renton Stadium, Seahawks Stadium (later renamed Qwest Field), and the Starfire Sports Complex in Tukwila, Washington. Highlights include four NASL Championships (1995, 1996, 2005, 2007).

November 13, 2007: Major League Soccer awards Seattle the league's 15th franchise and sets the team's debut for the 2009 season.

April 7, 2008: In the shadow of the Space Needle, the team's ownership group announces the team's name and colors. Seattle Sounders FC will wear rave green and Sounder blue.

I'm coming home to help the Sounders win, to
help the Sounders establish themselves as one
of the top franchises in the country . . .

—*Kasey Keller*

May 7, 2008: Sounders FC signs current USL Division 1 2007 MVP Sebastien Le Toux as its first player.

August 14, 2008: Sounders FC signs Washington native and world-class goalkeeper Kasey Keller as its second player.

December 5, 2008: Seattle unveils its complete home, away, and training kit collection at the Sounders FC Fashion Show held at the WaMu Theater.

March 27–31, 2008: Seattle fans participate in the "name the team" online vote. The club offers three options: Seattle Alliance, Seattle FC, and Seattle Republic. The fans kick off a write-in vote campaign to incorporate the name "Sounders," and more than 80 percent of the 15,000 votes cast propose a variation of the Sounders name.

May 28, 2008: Sounders FC announces a partnership with Microsoft's Xbox division and unveils the team's rave green home kit. Seattle Sounders FC jerseys will feature the Xbox 360 Live logo and Qwest Field's playing surface will be referred to as the "Xbox Pitch at Qwest Field."

October 28, 2008: Swedish International star Freddie Ljungberg joins Sounders FC as its designated player.

December 16, 2008: Sounders FC signs two-time MLS Cup Champion head coach Sigi Schmid.

March 19, 2009: Sounders FC plays its debut match before 32,523 fans on the Xbox Pitch at Qwest Field. The club claims its first franchise victory and match ticket sellout in a 3-0 win versus New York Red Bulls.

August 5, 2009: Sounders FC hosts FC Barcelona in an international friendly in front the largest crowd in Qwest Field history (66,848).

October 17, 2009: Sounders FC becomes the second MLS expansion team in history to qualify for the playoffs in its first season.

2009

July 18, 2009: Sounders FC hosts Chelsea FC in an international friendly in front of 65,289 fans at Qwest Field in Seattle.

September 2, 2009: With a 2-1 win over D.C. United, Sounders FC becomes the second MLS expansion team in league history to win the U.S. Open Cup.

November 22, 2009: Sounders FC hosts the MLS Cup at Qwest Field. 46,011 attend as Real Salt Lake wins the 2009 MLS Cup with a 5-4 penalty shootout victory over the LA Galaxy.

I think it's a great start for the franchise. It's a great start for us as owners to trust the fans, to show that we are about democracy in sports and set up situations in which fans have rights that they don't have with other American sports teams.

—*Sounders FC majority owner Joe Roth*

SEATTLE
SOUNDERS FC
2009 INAUGURAL SEASON ROSTER

OSVALDO ALONSO

6 | Midfielder

Born: November 11, 1985

Hometown: San Cristóbal, Cuba

How Acquired: Signed as free agent on January 26, 2009.

Previous Clubs: FC Pinar del Rio (Cuba, 2005–07), Charleston Battery (USL, 2008)

EVAN BROWN

16 | Defender

Born: May 1, 1987

Hometown: Raleigh, North Carolina

College: Wake Forest

How Acquired: Selected in the 2009 MLS SuperDraft on January 15, 2009.

BEN DRAGAVON

22 | Goalkeeper

Born: December 31, 1983

Hometown: Monroe, Washington

College: Western Washington

How Acquired: Part of the MLS league-wide reserve goalkeeper pool. Called up by Sounders FC in early 2009.

BRAD EVANS

3 | Midfielder

Born: April 20, 1985

Hometown: Phoenix, Arizona

College: UC Irvine

How Acquired: Selected from Columbus in the MLS Expansion Draft, November 26, 2008.

Previous Clubs: Columbus (MLS, 2007–08)

CHRIS EYLANDER

1 | Goalkeeper

Born: March 14, 1984

Hometown: Auburn, Washington

College: Washington

How Acquired: Signed as discovery player on January 5, 2009.

Previous Clubs: Seattle Sounders (USL-1, 2006–08)

KEVIN FORREST

19 | Forward

Born: November 3, 1984

Hometown: Seattle, Washington

College: Washington

How Acquired: Signed on March 24, 2009.

Previous Clubs: Colorado (MLS, 2008), Seattle (USL-1, 2008)

LEONARDO GONZALEZ

19 | Defender

Born: November 21, 1980

Hometown: San Jose, Costa Rica

How Acquired: Signed on July 2, 2009.

Previous Clubs: CS Herediano (Costa Rica, 2000–08), Municipal Liberia

TAYLOR GRAHAM

26 | Defender

Born: June 3, 1980

Hometown: Fair Oaks, California

College: Stanford

How Acquired: Signed as discovery player on January 21, 2009.

Previous Clubs: Kansas City (MLS, 2003–04), Seattle (USL, 2005), New York (MLS, 2006–07), Seattle Sounders (USL-1, 2007–08)

JHON KENNEDY HURTADO

34 | Defender

Born: May 16, 1984

Hometown: Palmira, Colombia

How Acquired: Signed as senior international player on February 18, 2009.

Previous Clubs: Unión Magdalena (Colombia, 2004), Monagas de Maturin (Colombia, 2005), Centauros Villavicencio (Colombia, 2006), Expreso Rojo (Colombia, 2006), Real Cartagena (Colombia, 2007), Deportivo Cali (Colombia, 2008–09)

PATRICK IANNI

4 | Defender

Born: June 15, 1985

Hometown: Lodi, California

College: UCLA

How Acquired: Acquired via trade from the Houston Dynamo on January 26, 2009.

Previous Clubs: Houston (MLS, 2006–08)

NATE JAQUA
21 | Forward
Born: October 28, 1981
Hometown: Eugene, Oregon
College: Portland (Oregon)
How Acquired: Selected from Houston in the MLS Expansion Draft on November 26, 2008.
Previous Clubs: Chicago (MLS, 2003–06), LA Galaxy (MLS, 2007), Houston (MLS, 2007), SC Rheindorf Altach (Austria, 2007–08), Houston (MLS, 2008)

KASEY KELLER
18 | Goalkeeper
Born: November 29, 1969
Hometown: Olympia, Washington
College: Portland (Oregon)
How Acquired: Signed as free agent on August 14, 2008, using MLS #1 allocation selection.
Previous Clubs: Millwall (England, 1992–96), Leicester City (England, 1996–99), Rayo Vallecano (Spain, 1999–2001), Tottentham (England, 2001–2004), Southampton (England, loan 2002–03), Borussia Mönchengladbach (Germany, 2004–07), Fulham (England, 2007–08)

STEPHEN KING
15 | Midfielder
Born: March 6, 1986
Hometown: Medford, New Jersey
College: Maryland
How Acquired: Selected from Chicago in MLS Expansion Draft on November 26, 2008.
Previous Clubs: Chicago (MLS, 2008)

SEBASTIEN LE TOUX
9 | Forward
Born: January 10, 1984
Hometown: Rennes, France
How Acquired: Purchased from USL-1 Sounders, May 8, 2008; loaned back for remainder of 2008 season.
Previous Clubs: FC Lorient (France, 2004–06), Seattle Sounders (USL-1, 2007–08)

ROGER LEVESQUE
24 | Forward
Born: January 22, 1981
Hometown: Portland, Maine
College: Stanford
How Acquired: Signed as discovery player on March 16, 2009
Previous Clubs: San Jose (MLS, 2003), Seattle Sounders (USL-1, 2004–08), San Jose (MLS, 2005)

FREDDIE LJUNGBERG

10 | Midfielder

Born: April 16, 1977

Hometown: Vittsjö, Sweden

College: Stanford

How Acquired: Signed as free agent designated player on October 28, 2008.

Previous Clubs: BK Halmstad (Sweden, 1994–98, Arsenal (England, 1998–2007), West Ham United (England (2007–08)

TYRONE MARSHALL

14 | Defender

Born: November 12, 1974

Hometown: Lauderhill, Florida

College: Florida International

How Acquired: Acquired by Seattle in trade with Toronto FC in exchange for allocation money on February 10, 2009.

Previous Clubs: Colorado (MLS, 1998), Miami (MLS, 1998–2001), LA Galaxy (MLS, 2002–07), Toronto (MLS, 2007–08)

FREDY MONTERO

17 | Forward

Born: July 26, 1987

Hometown: Campo de la Cruz, Colombia

How Acquired: Signed on loan January 21, 2009.

Previous Clubs: Deportivo Cali (Colombia, 2005–09), Atlético Huila (Colombia, loan 2007)

SANNA NYASSI

23 | Midfielder

Born: January 31, 1989

Hometown: Bwiam, Gambia

How Acquired: Signed as free agent September 5, 2008.

Previous Clubs: Seattle Sounders (USL-1, 2008)

JAMES RILEY

7 | Defender

Born: October 26, 1982

Hometown: Colorado Springs, Colorado

College: Wake Forest

How Acquired: Selected from San Jose in the MLS Expansion Draft, November 26, 2008.

Previous Clubs: New England (MLS, 2005–07), San Jose (MLS, 2008)

ZACH SCOTT

20 | Defender

Born: July 2, 1980

Hometown: Haiku, Hawaii

College: Gonzaga

How Acquired: Signed as discovery player on March 16, 2009.

Previous Clubs: Seattle Sounders (USL-1, 2002–08)

JARROD SMITH

13 | Forward

Born: June 10, 1984

Hometown: Havelock North, New Zealand

College: West Virginia

How Acquired: Selected from Toronto FC in the MLS Expansion Draft, November 26, 2008.

Previous Clubs: Toronto FC (MLS, 2007–08)

NATHAN STURGIS

12 | Defender/midfielder

Born: July 6, 1987

Hometown: St. Augustine, Florida

College: Clemson

How Acquired: Selected from Real Salt Lake in 2008 Expansion Draft, November 26, 2008.

Previous Clubs: LA Galaxy (MLS, 2006–07), Real Salt Lake (MLS, 2007–08)

PETER VAGENAS

8 | Midfielder

Born: February 6, 1978

Hometown: Pasadena, California

College: UCLA

How Acquired: Selected from Los Angeles in 2008 Expansion Draft. November 26, 2008.

Previous Club: LA Galaxy (MLS, 2000–08)

TYSON WAHL

5 | Defender

Born: February 23, 1984

Hometown: Newport Beach, California

College: California

How Acquired: Selected from Kansas City in the MLS Expansion Draft, November 26, 2008.

Previous Club: Kansas City (MLS, 2006–08)

STEVE ZAKUANI

11 | Forward

Born: February 9, 1988

Hometown: London, England

College: Akron

How Acquired: Selected with the first overall pick in the MLS SuperDraft, January 15, 2009.

BRIAN SCHMETZER

Assistant Coach

Experience: 8 years

Born: August 18, 1962

Hometown: Seattle, Washington

Joined Sounders: 2008

Previous Clubs: Head coach, Seattle Sounders (USL-1, 2002–08)

SIGI SCHMID

Head Coach

Experience: 8 years

Born: March 20, 1953

Hometown: Manhattan Beach, California

College: UCLA

Joined Sounders: 2008

Previous Clubs: LA Galaxy (MLS, 1999–2004), Columbus Crew (MLS, 2006–08)

SEATTLE SOUNDERS FC

2009 MLS REGULAR SEASON AND PLAYOFF RECORD

3/19/09	New York Red Bulls at Sounders FC	W	3-0
3/28/09	Real Salt Lake at Sounders FC	W	2-0
4/4/09	Toronto FC vs. Sounders FC	W	2-0
4/11/09	Kansas City Wizards at Sounders FC	L	0-1
4/18/09	Chivas USA vs. Sounders FC	L	0-2
4/25/09	San Jose Earthquakes at Sounders FC	W	2-0
5/2/09	Chicago Fire vs. Sounders FC	T	1-1
5/10/09	LA Galaxy at Sounders FC	T	1-1
5/16/09	FC Dallas vs. Sounders FC	T	1-1
5/23/09	Colorado Rapids vs. Sounders FC	T	2-2
5/30/09	Columbus Crew at Sounders FC	T	1-1
6/6/09	Chivas USA vs. Sounders FC	L	0-1
6/13/09	San Jose Earthquakes at Sounders FC	W	2-1
6/17/09	D.C. United at Sounders FC	T	3-3

6/20/09	New York Red Bulls vs. Sounders FC	T	1-1
6/28/09	Colorado Rapids at Sounders FC	W	3-0
7/11/09	Houston Dynamo at Sounders FC	W	2-1
7/25/09	Chicago Fire at Sounders FC	T	0-0
8/2/09	Earthquakes vs. Sounders FC	L	0-4
8/8/09	Real Salt Lake vs. Sounders FC	L	0-1
8/15/09	LA Galaxy vs. Sounders FC	W	2-0
8/20/09	New England Revolution at Sounders FC	L	0-1
8/23/09	Houston Dynamo vs. Sounders FC	T	1-1
8/29/09	Toronto FC at Sounders FC	T	0-0
9/12/09	D.C. United vs. Sounders FC	W	2-1
9/19/09	Chivas USA at Sounders FC	T	0-0
9/26/09	New England Revolution vs. Sounders FC	L	1-2
10/3/09	Columbus Crew vs. Sounders FC	W	1-0
10/17/09	Kansas City Wizards vs. Sounders FC	W	3-2
10/24/09	FC Dallas at Sounders FC	W	2-1
10/29/09	Western Conference Playoff Leg One: Houston Dynamo at Sounders FC	T	0-0
11/8/09	Western Conference Playoff Leg Two: Houston Dynamo vs. Sounders FC	L	0-1 OT

Overall Record
12 wins, 7 ties, 11 losses

Final Standing
3rd place, Western Conference

Total Points
47

SEATTLE SOUNDERS FC
SUPPORTER GROUPS

EMERALD CITY SUPPORTERS

Emerald City Supporters (ECS) consists of a group of independent supporters of Seattle Sounders FC. The ECS was formed in 2005. Back then, we supported the now-defunct Seattle Sounders of USL Division 1. We look at Seattle Sounders FC as a direct continuation of that same soccer tradition. To join ECS, just show up in our section at Qwest Field. We stand in the south end general admission sections 121–123, also nicknamed the Brougham End. Before home games a lot of us will also gather at Fuel, a bar just a couple of blocks north of Qwest Field.

During the off-season, sign up on our discussion forum and attend one of the off-season events that will be announced there at *www.weareecs.com*.

SEATTLE GORILLA FC

Seattle Gorilla FC (GFC) welcomes futbol fans (soccer fans too). We are an Antifa supporters group of the Sounders FC actively working against racism/sexism and homophobia. If you like to party, then this is the supporter club you're looking for. We are dedicated to the Seattle Sounders FC and the party that goes with that devotion—drinking, chanting, drumming, and screaming our lungs out at every game! Gorilla FC sits in sections 119 and 120 at the south end of Qwest

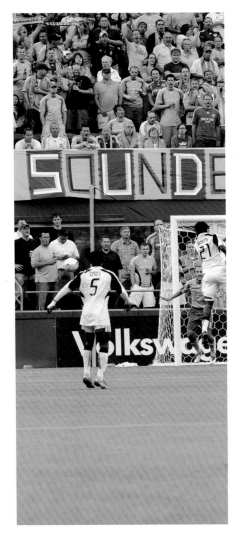

Field. We meet at Fado Irish Pub before every game and march together closer to game time. For 2010, Gorilla FC's membership fee is $20 and includes the GFC 2010 scarf. Your membership scarf will get you specials at Fado, Elysian Fields, the Dray, and our other partner locations.

Join up now and enjoy the community and the party benefits at *www.gorillafc.com*.

NORTH END SUPPORTERS

North End Supporters (NES) is a Sounders FC supporter group located at the north end of Qwest Field. If you like to stand, chant, sing, wave flags, and hold up scarves while creating a positive and intense atmosphere, then the NES is the home for you! We aim to fill the north end of Qwest Field with the loudest, proudest, and most loyal fans of the Sounders FC. With the use of songs, chants, drums, horns, flags, banners, scarves, and other festive techniques, we promise to cheer on our beloved Sounders FC and rattle the nerves of our opponents when they're near our end of the stadium. Our primary locations include the all-inclusive sections 100 and 144–152, as well as the upper sections of 100, 101, 102, 142, and 144 (and expanding).

Learn more about us at *www.northendsupporters.com*.

SEATTLE
SOUNDERS FC
BLOGGERS

Goal Seattle
David Falk

www.goalseattle.com
www.twitter.com/seattlesoccer

David Falk has followed Seattle soccer since 1974. There is no bigger or better archive of Sounders and Seattle soccer history than the museum hosted at *GOALSeattle.com*. David became the soccer beat writer for *Examiner.com* in 2008.

Prost Amerika
Steve Clare

www.prostamerika.com
www.twitter.com/prostsoccer

Prost Amerika is Seattle's only award-winning soccer site. As well as providing the best match reports, it covers the world of soccer from a Seattle perspective. Steve Clare also co-hosts the Radio Sounders podcast.

Rave Green
Matt Gaschk

www.soundersfc.com/news/blogs
www.twitter.com/soundersfc

Rave Green is the official insider blog of the Seattle
Sounders FC maintained by Matt Gaschk, the site's
head writer and online host. The *SoundersFC.com*
community has more than 4,500 users in addition to
55,000 Facebook fans and more than 2,000 Twitter
followers.

Seattle Times
Jose Romero

www.seattletimes.nwsource.com/html/soundersfcblog
www.twitter.com/mividadeportiva

Jose Miguel Romero of the *Seattle Times* left the
Seahawks beat after the 2008 season to get in on the
ground floor of the Sounders FC. He covered the team
on a daily basis in 2009, traveled to more than half the
team's road games, and enjoyed every minute of it.

Sounder at Heart
Dave Clark

www.sounderatheart.com
www.twitter.com/sounderatheart

Sounder at Heart provides analysis of players, tactics, and trends for Sounders FC and Major League Soccer, with forays into democracy in sports. Dave also serves on the Alliance Council, representing fans around the stadium and region.

Sounders Fan Insider
Greg Roth

www.soundersfaninsider.net
www.twitter.com/soundersfi

Sounders Fan Insider serves the Puget Sound, United States, and global soccer community by supporting, promoting, and evangelizing the beautiful game through insight into the Seattle Sounders FC's organization, players' rich histories, community service activities, supporter groups, and fans.